MOTORISTS G...

West...
Peakl...

JACK HANMER

Willow
PUBLISHING

© Willow Publishing 1980
ISBN 9506043 3 X

Willow Publishing,
Willow Cottage, 36 Moss Lane,
Timperley, Altrincham,
Cheshire, WA15 6SZ.

Photography and illustrations
by Keith Warrender.

Printed by The Commercial Centre Ltd.,
Clowes Street, Hollinwood, Oldham.

Cover photograph: Lyme Hall
Opposite: Errwood Reservoir, Goyt Valley

Contents

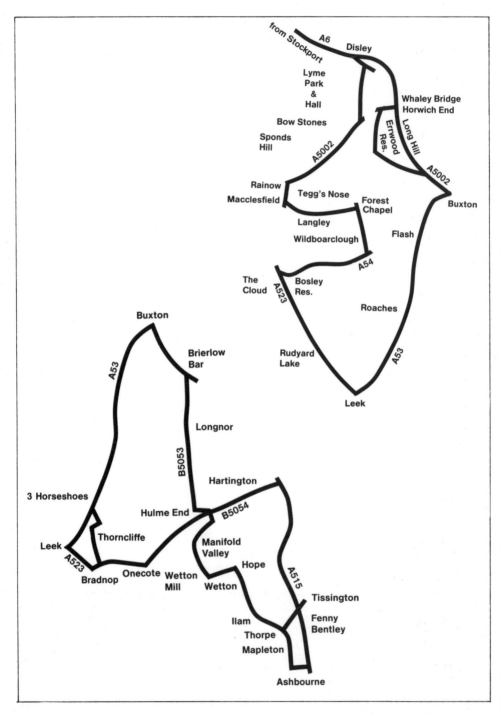

1
Around Western Peakland

This first section puts the whole area of Western Peakland into perspective by suggesting two fairly comprehensive whistle-stop tours. If you are very ambitious you could combine the two but this would savour too much of a timed motor-club rally. The intention is to let you sample the region at two sittings so to speak so that you will become familiar with the geography of the place — orientated in fact.

To discover from the text that Hulme End for example, is visited some four or five times is likely to cause some confusion. When you realise its strategic position in relation to a number of the sections then all becomes clear. The two routes described will occasionally run counter to the directions in the separate sections. This will enable you to see much of the area from a different angle when views from the opposite approach are sometimes missed.

Getting the feel of the place before actually coming to grips with it is a useful preliminary. Do not therefore be tempted to linger too long on these initial tours. Rather, follow them in their entirety then, over a period of time explore Western Peakland at your leisure and to your delight. The first starts at Disley on the A6 and the second at Buxton, also on the same trunk road.

Leave Disley by Buxton Old Road, behind the Ram's Head, turn right for Kettleshulme with the Macclesfield sign on Mudhurst Lane. This road runs round the southern boundary of Lyme Park with the Cage on the horizon. At the left turn for Moorfield is the right fork for Bowstones Gate and the view point on Sponds Hill. The road ahead continues to Kettleshulme and then Macclesfield via Rainow village and the various diversions to Jenkin Chapel, Lamaload Reservoir, etc. From Macclesfield the Leek and the Langley roads take you to Langley, Tegg's Nose Country Park and Macclesfield Forest with its Chapel. Along now through Wildboarclough to the A54 and the right turn for Congleton, skirting the Wincle/Danebridge area as far as Bosley crossroads. Take the Leek road now with first, The Cloud rising across to your right, then, after Rushton Spencer, the expanse of Rudyard Lake down

Chapel House Cheddleton

below you. In Leek you could collect some appropriate leaflets from the Information Centre in St Edward's Street before leaving on the A53 for the twelve mile run back to Buxton. This moorland road is your reference point for a number of interesting attractions which lie on both sides of the route. In Buxton you can return via the A6, that's Fairfield Common, Dove Holes and Chapel-en-le-Frith, or the more popular Long Hill, the A5002. Both meet at Horwich End and continue as the A6 to Disley, Stockport and Manchester.

The second whistle-stop tour begins in Buxton and follows the Ashbourne road, the A515 to Brierlow Bar, where you take the right fork for Longnor. The B5053 runs through Longnor towards Warslow but turn left by the white painted railings for Hulme End and there take stock for a moment by the Light Railway Hotel. The road by the pub runs into the Manifold Valley, the one behind you running south continues to Warslow and the Staffordshire moorland villages of Onecote and Ipstones, then Froghall. The road ahead is your onward route to Hartington, a very popular tourist centre for country lovers of all kinds. From Hartington go ahead past the old station with its Information Centre in the signal box and join the A515 again to travel south. Tissington can be circumnavigated by entering the estate at the first approach left, running through the village and re-joining the A515 where the road opposite runs on to Thorpe and Dovedale. This cuts out Ashbourne if you are running short of time since Thorpe and Ilam are on the forward route in any case.

Should you decide to visit Ashbourne the local Information Centre can supply you with yet more leaflets — be sure to pick up one on the Peak Pathfinder bus service. Now make for Mapleton village to reach Thorpe and Ilam where you begin the tours of both Dovedale and the Manifold Valley (Sections 9 and 10). Make for Alstonfield but turn off for Wetton at Hopedale and descend to the Manifold Valley and the road out through the old Swainsley Railway Tunnel (west, through the tunnel, now a roadway). After Ecton this brings you back to Hulme End where you turn left on the B5054 for Warslow and Onecote (Oncote). In Onecote turn right for Bradnop and Leek but note first the road ahead to the junction with the A523 at Bottom House. This is the onward route to Ipstones, Froghall, Cheddleton, Alton and the Churnet Valley.

In Bradnop turn right on to the A523, run into Leek and take again the A53 to Buxton. Alternatively, a cross-country route which by-passes Leek leaves Bradnop village for Thorncliffe where in that village you turn left, pass behind the Army Camp and join the Buxton road by the Three Horseshoes Inn at Blackshaw Moor. Climb up past The Roaches and then on over Axe Edge to Buxton.

Hartington signal box

Right: Whaley Bridge wharf

2
Lyme Park, Kettleshulme, Pott Shrigley, Bollington, Macclesfield, Prestbury, Adlington Hall.

It is no coincidence that this first detailed section transports you from the hurly-burly of city and town to the perimeter of wild moorland scenery. The transition is gradual, beginning as it does in parkland before moving on to more open country. It is an area of contrasts: two great houses, mill towns and stockbroker belts, flat, fertile agricultural plains and bleak moors.

The busy A6 trunk road passes the entrance to Lyme Hall and Park between High Lane and Disley and a 'train' ride up the long drive might appeal to the children. This is your first opportunity to spot the herd of red deer which roam the Park. Owned by the National Trust and administered by Stockport Corporation, Lyme Park is in itself a day out. The Hall in parts dates from 1541 and the whole estate was originally in the hands of the Legh family. For the active young there's a challenging play area and a Nature Trail and for the active old a number of walks or rounds which conveniently bring you back to the car park! Actually, it's more interesting and sometimes exciting to let someone drive the car to a convenient rendezvous — in this case either Bow Stones beyond Higher Disley or the canal at Higher Poynton. Leaflets for the Nature Trail and some of the walks are available at the information hut.

The view from Bow Stones is panoramic to say the least, stretching as it does across the northern end of the Cheshire Plain. Woodford Aerodrome is in the foreground and Ringway towards Altrincham are but two of the landmarks — Jodrell Bank being another.

To reach Kettleshulme from this back road which is east of Lyme Park a pleasant diversion runs off left, after the 'cattle' sign and crosses the Todd Brook before climbing to the village. On this stretch too, stands an old candlewick mill with cottages and tumbling mill-race to complete the picture. The mill is now occupied by a craftsman who restores ironwork in the shape of gates lamp posts and the like. From Charles Head, after Kettleshulme, a minor road off right descends to Pott Shrigley, unfortunately the less picturesque of the several approaches to this charming village. The quarry workings of a former brick works and the more recent chemical

Tower, Kerridge Hill.

industry have little in common with the peace and quiet of this tiny hamlet.

The Parish Church is appropriately St Christopher's, the Patron Saint of travellers and the millstone grit fabric is unusual for a Cheshire church. Pott Shrigley which intrigues most has an interesting derivation: Pott is both a family name and old English for a tarn or pool; Shrigley was shriggel or shriggeleg — a wood frequented by shrikes. I have it on good authority that there are none lying in wait for today's traveller!

Bollington is a former mill town which like many of its contemporaries now houses a variety of industries in its still satanic mills. Two features dominate the town; a twenty arch railway viaduct and White Nancy. The latter is not a puritanical maiden but a pillar erected on high ground at Kerridge to commemorate the battle of Waterloo. In Bollington locate Jackson's Lane, then Redway Lane for Kerridge and White Nancy which can be reached by path for a closer look. From the Redway Tavern follow the minor road, Windmill Lane, round to its junction with the A5002 and turn right for Macclesfield.

White Nancy

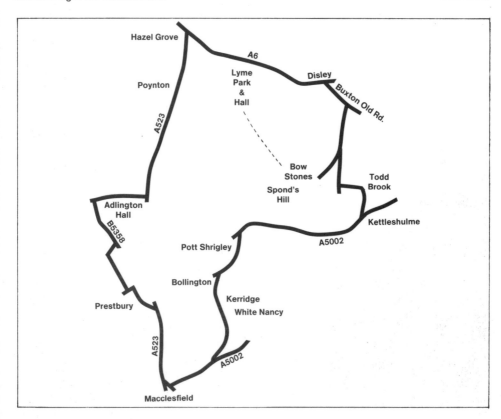

This is the only sizeable town in this northern section and has a tradition of silk manufacturing. The central landmark is St Michael's, the Parish Church, with an assortment of relics which not unnaturally have some connection with the Legh family. A word here about churches would not be amiss since the whole region is dotted with ecclesiastical buildings of various denominations. The old tag 'when you've seen one you've seen them all' is very definitely not the case with churches for each has its own characteristics. They range from the impressive St Michael's at Macclesfield to the much smaller Jenkin Chapel below Kettleshulme with a variety of shapes and sizes in between.

To return to Macclesfield, the town has not suffered dramatically at the hands of the planners who have achieved an acceptable merger of the old with the new. For bowls enthusiasts West Park has an extremely large crown green and also monoliths, supposedly Saxon stones. A particularly large glacial stone gives rise to much speculation as to its origin and the museum and art gallery at the park's entrance contains some fine pictures and an Egyptian collection.

Prestbury lies north of Macclesfield off the A523 and is generally thought to be stockbroker country, though famous sportsmen and television personalities also find it a congenial habitat. The village is noted for its restaurants and it is a delight simply to promenade down the village street to admire the architecture. There cannot be many places where it would be a positive pleasure to have an overdraft in a bank with such charm! To reach Adlington from Prestbury take the minor road opposite the station, pass (swiftly) the sewage works, turn left on to the B5258 and at the T junction turn right for Adlington Hall. This again is part of the Legh family estates and architecturally it combines the traditional black and white portion of the late sixteenth century with Georgian sections and further additions as recent as the 1920's. Its claim to fame lies in the great organ on which Handel is reputed not only to have played but composed the Harmonious Blacksmith. Time was when the Hall was a hunting lodge in Macclesfield Forest which is now considerably reduced in size. From the Hall run on to the main road, then turn left for Hazel Grove and the A6.

Anything/which relates to 'The Peak District' automatically suggests Derbyshire so you may be surprised to discover that much of this first section lies in Cheshire. The confusion does not end there for in another section the famous Three Shires Heads refers to Cheshire, Derbyshire and Staffordshire! No-one it seems has a monopoly on the Peak District. This handy reference summarizes, your route:

The A6 to Lyme Park then Disley; Buxton Old Road behind the Ram's Head to Higher Disley and Kettleshulme;

Pott Shrigley Church

at Moorfield Hotel sign fork right for Bow Stones; park and continue to end of track to Sponds Hill triangulation point for best view; back on Kettleshulme road, by-road off left (the only one) to back of Kettleshulme and old mill; turn right after climbing out of Kettleshulme for Pott Shrigley and Bollington; White Nancy is behind the Redway Tavern at Kerridge; Windmill Lane to A5002 then right for Macclesfield; the A523 Manchester road out of Macclesfield to Prestbury turn for that village; after seeing village take minor road opposite station, left past sewage works to B5358 to T junction and right for Adlington Hall; at main road A523 turn left for Hazel Grove and A6.

Prestbury

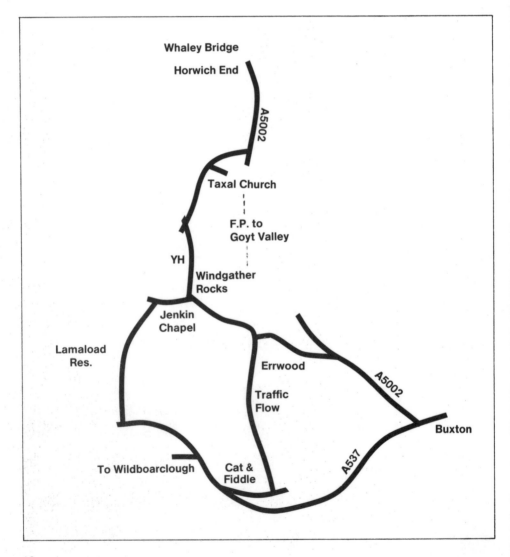

3
Whaley Bridge, Goyt Valley, Buxton, Jenkin Chapel.

Whaley Bridge again on the A6, is the springboard for this section but before embarking on its main course you might care to take a closer look at the town itself. Whaley Bridge attracts watermen of two distinct types: the sailing people on Toddbrook Reservoir and the canal enthusiasts who frequent the basin and terminus of an arm of the Peak Forest Canal. This location was also the terminus of the old Cromford and High Peak Railway which enthusiasts would dearly love to have seen operating. What a tourist attraction this would have been in an age which appears to thrive on the historical and the nostalgic. You can read all about it in the canal shop which also houses an assortment of historical items.

Historically Whaley Bridge has to be appreciated on foot and it is an easy matter to follow the first section of the old Cromford and High Peak Railway from the transit shed at the canal basin. The route passes the car park, crosses the Goyt (note the old lever for throwing the points), then climbs the now tree lined incline to the Old Road where is located an old air shaft of a former coal mine.

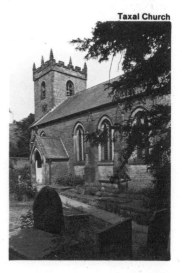

Taxal Church

Down on the main road, the A6 and behind The Cock Hotel is a path leading up to the present B R main line and the skew tunnel of the old line. By continuing and crossing the A6 again you pass Cromford Court and at the Taxal Scout Hut is the Shallcross Incline where walking now becomes hazardous. Along the A6 to Horwich End the Macclesfield Road, the A5002 begins to climb in the direction of Taxal and the Goyt Valley. Taxal Lodge is a special school whilst the church, the Chimes Inn and a few farmsteads make up the hamlet itself. This is the start of an invigorating slightly uphill walk along the Goyt Valley passing first the old then the more recent reservoir, the latter being Errwood with still more sailing.

To drive into the Goyt Valley take the first left after the Taxal turns and climb up past the Youth Hostel at Windgather Rocks which are nursery slopes for climbers. At the T junction the road, right runs on to Jenkin Chapel and Kettleshulme and this is your return route later. Now turn left into the Goyt Valley which has an experimental traffic system along its more popular scenic length. On Sundays and Bank Holiday Mondays cars must be parked and a ride taken by mini-bus to avoid congestion. (On week days the route is a one way system in this direction.) The 'escape route' if one is required, is to skirt the reservoir and climb out of the Valley to the famous Long Hill, the A5002, and on into Buxton. The incline on this stretch was formerly part of the High Peak Railway line. If the run up the Goyt Valley itself is made this follows the new section of road above the reservoir passing a number of picturesque picnic spots and the site of the old Errwood Hall. This community once contained its own school, coalmine, mill and cemetery, but alas, has now nothing to show except colourful rhododendrons and azaleas amongst its foundations.

It was built around 1830 by the Grimshawe family but exactly one hundred years later ceased to be a private residence and was eventually demolished when the lower, Fernilee, reservoir was completed in 1938. The Errwood reservoir was completed in 1967 and thoughtfully the Water Board re-erected the old packhorse bridge upstream near Goytsclough Quarry. This had been a salt smugglers route in the days of the salt tax.

Old Errwood Hall

The Crescent, Buxton

Buxton is the main town in this section and, of course, its fame has sprung from its springs. The mineral water which lies some three to five thousand feet deep and which surfaces at the rate of 200,000 gallons a day was considered by the Romans to have medicinal qualities. So much so that a mere eighteen centuries later the fifth Duke of Devonshire developed the town as a rival to Bath. One of his legacies was the famous Crescent and the Great Stables, now transformed into the Devonshire Royal Hospital with its elegant unsupported Dome spanning 156 feet. Any tour of Buxton should begin at St Anne's Well opposite The Crescent. A sample of the famous mineral water may be taken but perhaps more important, the Information Centre is also housed here and absolutely everything one could wish to know about Buxton and its surrounds is available in some leaflet or other.

Two attractions which demand an element of walking are Pool's Cavern and Solomon's Temple, the latter visible for quite some distance. Corbar Crags and Wood also contain pleasant walks with the added bonus of charming views of the town from a number of vantage points. The museum in Terrace Road on the way up to the Market Place contains the usual assortment of historical bric-a-brac plus, of course, vestiges of the Roman occupation. There are three major routes running across wild moorland south of Buxton; to Leek the A53, to Congleton the A54 and to Macclesfield, but not the A55 as one would suppose

but the A537, the Cat and Fiddle route and the beginning of Section 4.

The Cat andFiddle on the A537 is your reference point now and you have either travelled up through the Goyt Valley (week days only) or approached it via Buxton and the Macclesfield road. Continuing to Macclesfield notice the road which falls away left to Wildboarclough, but ignore this for the moment and at the crossroads with the sign Saltersford three miles, turn right for Lamaload Reservoir. This is a switchback road both before and after the picnic site at Hooley Hay where you can relax and picnic if your timing or the inner man suggests that you should. After the picnic site take the right fork for Jenkin Chapel which is now visible across the valley. This eighteenth century church is in fact St John's, Saltersford, but more commonly called Jenkin Chapel and holds services on the second and fourth Sundays in the month at 3.00 pm. It is situated on The Street, that same route familiar to salt smuggling tax dodgers.

The return route lies ahead to the entrance to the Goyt Valley where you turn left and descend to Taxal and Whaley Bridge. Your first turn right after the Youth Hostel is probably not signed — it's a narrow road and maybe the way ahead is slightly less of a problem. Either way you meet the A5002 and turn right for Whaley Bridge and the A6.

4
Tegg's Nose Country Park, Wildboarclough, Gawsworth.

The northern boundary of this section is the Buxton/Macclesfield road and the whole area is a pleasant mixture of two differing types of terrain: the lusher pastures of Cheshire around Gawsworth and the more rugged but equally interesting scenery bordering Axe Edge.

The remains of a once great forest, another tucked away Chapel, a developing country park, a clough with a name which leaves no-one in doubt and a beautiful black and white hall are all contained within this narrow compass.

At first sight one might suppose that an area only eight miles across and at most eight miles deep could hardly hold one's attention for long. The fact that these seemingly small sections do just that is proof enough that they contain a wealth of beauty and interest.

Langley, which is the location of Tegg's Nose Country Park and some vigorous walking can be reached either from the Leek road, the A523 or from off the old Buxton road about a mile after it leaves the A537.

Tegg's Nose Country Park

The Former Post Office at Wildbearclough

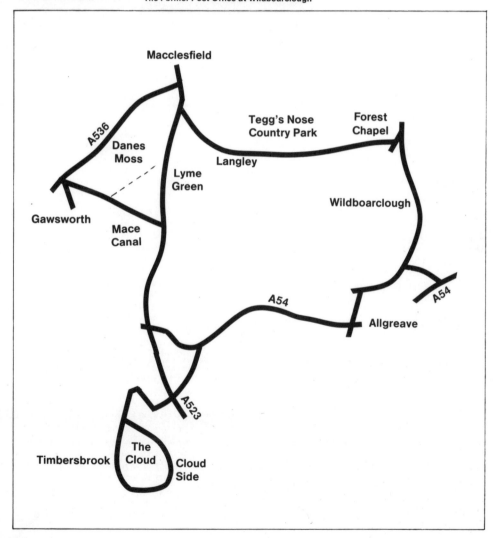

Macclesfield

A536

Danes Moss

Tegg's Nose Country Park

Forest Chapel

Langley

Lyme Green

Wildboarclough

Gawsworth

Mace Canal

A54

A54

Allgreave

A523

Timbersbrook

The Cloud

Cloud Side

Forest Chapel

Gawsworth

Tegg's Nose is signposted and should be visited before embarking on the run through Macclesfield Forest and Wildboarclough which likewise is well signed. The 17th Century "chapel in the forest" has an annual rush-bearing ceremony and the date is always publicised. The minor roads which traverse the forest skirt the small reservoirs and bring you to the very popular Wildboarclough, where, it is said, the last wild boar to be hunted perished.

If Tegg's Nose has been too much of a challenge, then one of the forest walks or the clough itself might salve your conscience. Charity Lane by Forest Chapel is such a walk which will take you to Walker Barn on the A537 where possibly a rendezvous with the car could be arranged.

In the clough itself the road meanders alongside the brook and there are a couple of hostelries for the thirsty or hungry. Where habitation is evident (Edinburgh Cottages seem to have lost their way) turn left for a few yards by the Church and note the building which was once the village Post Office. The size bore no resemblance to its volume of business for it was previously part of a carpet mill. Though quite large, it does not look out of place in this setting.

To leave the Clough continue to the main Congleton road by ignoring the minor road right and at the A54 take extreme care before turning right onto it. This is another switchback route which climbs and dips and, for a few miles forms the boundary of the National Park. Between the two minor roads running off right in the direction of Langley and Sutton is Cleulow Cross, the remains of an 11th century Saxon Cross. On the descent to Bosley Cross Roads and about one and a half miles from them is a left turn down to Bosley reservoir and the Leek road which you cross for the ascent to the Cloud. With the sign Timbersbrook 3 miles you first drive through the yard of the wood treatment plant, cross the Dane and climb to the road junction where a stile invites you to explore the Cloud. This is National Trust property with both easy and difficult walks and breathtaking views. With binoculars the peculiar outline of Mow Cop Folly can be more clearly defined though the naked eye will suffice to span the eight miles from the Cloud to the radio telescope at Jodrell Bank.

To complete the circuit of the Cloud so as to return to the junction at Red Lane continue to Timbersbrook. Here a country park is being developed by the authorities. Take the Biddulph road then the next left at the crossroads and pass "Bridestones" a name associated with a neolithic burial chamber and much more recently a splendid house. Another left turn brings you to Red Lane running along Cloud Side with yet more views. Descend to the Dane, the timber yard and the Leek road where you turn left for your return journey. On an aquatic note the O.S. Map at this point shows not only the river, but lists canal, locks, aqueduct, waterfall, weir and even moat!

The A523 crosses the A54 then some three miles further north is your minor road off left and over the Macclesfield Canal to Gawsworth, which is a delightful village. With two halls for good measure, a lovely church, a lake and statues of former Prime Ministers tucked away as though hiding, Gawsworth has that air of tranquillity we all seek at frequent intervals.

The older 15th century black and white hall has achieved a compromise by qualifying for the lower divisions of the Stately Homes League, whilst retaining an atmosphere of being lived in. Mary Fitton who once lived at the Hall, is thought to be the dark lady of Shakespeare's Sonnets. A small exhibition of carriages, including an ancient fire-engine will interest most people. The rather grotesque gargoyles which the Church displays will also interest, though possibly scare others. And still on the subject of carvings, the statues mentioned earlier would have been lost or destroyed but for the intervention of the owner of the Hall who rescued them.

The more modern, in fact, New Hall across the lake is owned by the County Council. Whichever way you turn in Gawsworth there appears to be something to photograph.

For the walker there is an interesting walk across part of Danes Moss, once a "deep and extensive peat bog". Although long since worked out, the track of the old tramway remains and the path eventually crosses the main line and on to the canal and Lyme Green where a rendezvous could be arranged.

A circular tour of the area which embraces all these attractions might well begin in Macclesfield itself or on the Buxton road. First make for Langley Village then Tegg's Nose from which there are two routes through the forest. The one straight ahead after the pub brings you to Forest Chapel and the head of Wildboarclough which is best travelled from north to south. At the A54 turn towards Congleton but take the slip road left for Bosley Reservoir and the Leek road. Cross the major road for the circuit of the Cloud, return to Bosley and turn north for Gawsworth then Macclesfield and home.

Gawsworth Hall

5

Three Shires Head, Lud's Church, Flash, The Roaches, Leek, Rudyard Lake, Danebridge.

In common with the last section the terrain here ranges from the rocky Roaches — wallaby land — to the more inviting Rudyard. Amongst its attractions are; the hidden location of secret worshippers, and the former haunt of counterfeiters.

Allgreave at the southern end of Wildboarclough would serve as a convenient reference point. It lies on the A54 at the junction of the Quarnford road which is the route to follow. Just before Gradbach, in fact a few yards beyond the farmhouse offering afternoon teas, is a gated road running off left leading to the location of Three Shires Head.

Panniers Pool Bridge

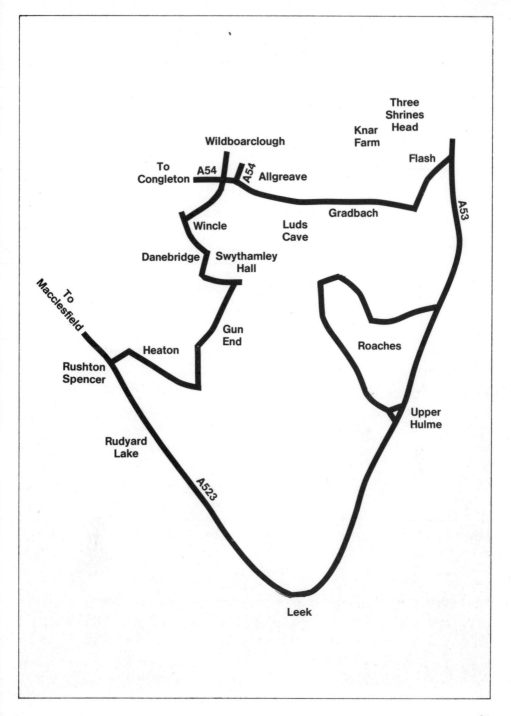

To reach Panniers Pool Bridge, to give it its true name, you should park at Knar Farm and walk down to the Dane, and then upstream to the bridge. Back at the Allgreave road, the sharp left turn is tricky and a better turn is by the farmhouse ahead. Here also is a shorter approach to the hidden Lud's Church, though the more usual route is as follows: continue past Gradbach Chapel, cross the Dane and turn right into the old mill yard; park by the gate and continue on foot. There's a certain sense of achievement in actually locating this geological phenomenon without more precise directions, save to say that the current OS Sheet 119 has it clearly marked. Historically the cave is best remembered for its connection with persecuted worshippers, though outlaws and rebels have also taken refuge in the secret rift.

Return to the minor road and continue ahead but ignore the Royal Cottage turn and continue to Flash. In spite of more common usage, Flash village is named after the counterfeit money, usually pewter, for which the area was once noted. Another claim lies in it height and the local pub is one of many reputed to be 'the highest in England'. At 1500 feet the Parish Church is also in on the act and no doubt justifiably for surely no other, Anglican or otherwise, can be so elevated, physically that is. Turn right on to the Buxton/Leek road, the A53, which has a reputation for mist and can be rather eerie for travellers at night. On clear days The Roaches dominate the skyline majestically and from this vantage point can be viewed various reservoirs, the towns of Congleton and Leek, the peculiar outline of Mow Cop, The Cloud and again the meanderings of the Dane. Unless you are an experienced climber it is

Lud's Church

Flash

not advisable to go scaling these rocks which have been acquired by the National Park Authority. The name Les Roches (The Rocks) was first given to the outcrop by French prisoners of the Napoleonic Wars.

Hen Cloud at 1250 feet is the most impressive of these gritstone outcrops and 'under its wing' lies the hamlet of Upper Hulme with Meerbrook village and the Tittesworth reservoir lying over towards Leek. The other fascinating feature of this area are the wallabies which, having escaped from a private zoo, have survived some thirty years of wintry Peakland weather. They are not easily visible, though binoculars and a degree of patience would help. Their exact location is not willingly given since the preservation of those which remain is of much concern.

Leek is a market town with that slowness of pace which commends itself, particularly to a city dweller. An informative Tourist Information Office will help you to plan future excursions into Staffordshire and a series of Leisure Drives in leaflet form are available. St Edward Street where the Tourist Office is located has some fine houses dating from the eighteenth century and at the traffic lights in Broad Street are the almshouses founded in the late seventeenth century by Elizabeth Ash. James Brindley, canal builder extraordinary, built a corn mill in Leek now restored and open to visitors.

Brindley's Corn Mill

North of Leek on the Macclesfield road, the A523, is Rudyard Lake and in keeping with tradition, you must be informed that one J L Kipling, the Stoke-on-Trent city architect, did his courting around the lake. Later in India, his son was born and christened, for sentimental reasons, 'Rudyard'. There is a walk around the lake which incidentally, was built to supply water to the Macclesfield Canal.

From Rudyard to Allgreave is one of those treasure-hunt type cross country routes which will challenge the map minded and confuse the others. On a philosophical note, getting lost is never a problem in Peakland, you will eventually arrive somewhere and thus be able to pick up your route and by way of a bonus probably see something you would have missed had you not got lost in the first place.

Rudyard Lake

Using OS Sheet 119 thread your way from the back of Rushton Spencer through Heaton to Swythamley and down to Danebridge, a delightful village much frequented by tourists both for the views and possibly the trout. Climb now to Wincle and in that village a right turn will bring you back to the Buxton/Congleton road, the A54, right opposite the road into Wildboarclough. Turn right for Buxton, or left for Congleton if you prefer a more direct route home.

By following the text in this section a circular tour which embraces all the attractions can be enjoyed. The time worn catch phrase 'all tastes catered for' is certainly applicable here.

6
Poole's Cavern, Hollinsclough, Longnor, Axe Edge.

With the possible exception of Buxton and its environs and also Hollinsclough, this region suffers from the handicap of having no "attractions" in the popular sense. Its appeal is directed chiefly at the walker and the naturalist, but it does also afford several opportunities for the townsman to appreciate the peace and quiet of the countryside.

Buxton and Harpur Hill should be explored first and in a clockwise direction to assist your onward route. Leave Buxton on the A515 Ashbourne road but at the bottom of the first dip and opposite the popular Duke's Drive turn right for Harpur Hill.

The College of Further Education in these parts has a catering department which has trained and sent students to ply their trade in most holiday resorts and well-known hotels.

Quarnford

Between the Post Office and the Parks Inn is Grin Low Road to the right and lying off left some half a mile along is a small industrial estate with as wide a range of establishments as you could imagine. A government mines research station, a cheese maturing warehouse and a car repairers are all on the same site! Continuing along Grin Low Road and near its junction with the Leek road is a footpath right leading to Solomon's Temple. There is no biblical connection here for like the splendid McCaig's Tower above lovely Oban in Scotland, this too was built by unemployed men at the end of the 19th century, in this case by one Solomon Mycock. How acceptable, one wonders, would such philanthropic schemes be today?

Solomon's Temple

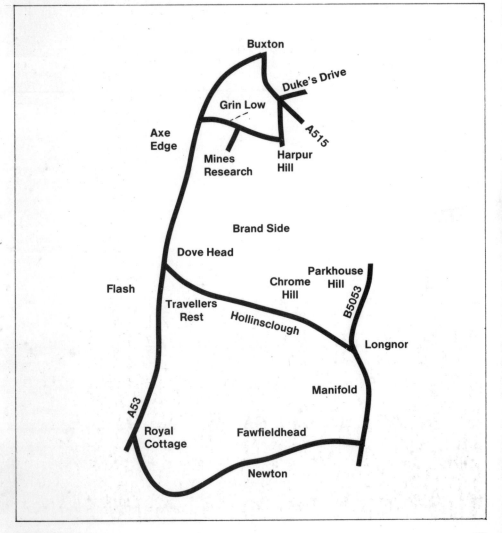

Chrome Hill and Parkhouse Hill

Incidentally Poole's Cavern which lies on the Buxton side of Grin Low is once again open to the public (older guides will refer to its closure).

The notorious rogue Poole not only knew the way into the cave but, and this was his salvation, he also knew a secret way out! One of the sources of the River Wye is contained here and the Cavern is certainly worth a visit.

The Low itself is carboniferous limestone which contains fossils and encrinites. At the Leek road the A53 turn left for the wild and rugged route across the moors passing Axe Edge on your right.

At the Travellers' Rest and the local store go on the minor road signed Longnor. Ignore the right fork and venture along the road signed "unsuitable for motors" which is quite safe, the only real hazard being oncoming traffic. The road dips through Moor Side and tracks run off in all directions to small holdings scattered about the hillsides. Looking north towards Buxton is first Brand Side and then Axe Edge but ahead lies one of those secret places often read about but never found.

Whichever way you approach Hollinsclough you are rewarded with a "surprise" view in that it is upon you before you know it. From the east, the approach you are now making, the twin peaks on the left are Hollins Hill and

Chrome (pronounced Croom) Hill in that order.

There is an interesting geological feature here in that whereas Hollins is gritstone, Chrome is Limestone. Further evidence is provided by the field walls which are constructed of both stones.

This marks a division of these two rock formations and the scenery has a positive link with whichever rock lies under the surface. The clough is best appreciated on foot when you will observe the more recent but less aesthetic Primary School. The older building is not likely to fall into decay having been adapted by one of the city comprehensives as a field study centre. Hollinsclough, like Elkstone in the next section, has an air of "mañana" about it and urban dwellers often make the false assumption that the twentieth century has not yet arrived in these parts. Television aerials usually kill that myth and as one local wag has it: "You're really quite safe here, we haven't eaten a missionary since goodness knows when!"

Whilst still on foot you might care to compete with the local schoolchildren who once listed over three hundred different kinds of wild flower in and around the place. If walking is your particular forte you could locate the cave in Dowel Dale where New Stone Age relics have been found. The cave lies in the dale behind Chrome Hill and before Parkhouse Hill.

Take the left fork out of the Clough (the 'phone box being on the right fork) and after the climb, park conveniently, then walk back to the "surprise view" which greets you from the Western approach.

At the major road the B5053, turn right run through Longnor and out on the Warslow road, still the B5053. After crossing the Manifold climb to the cross roads and turn right for Fawfieldhead. The old building now used as a garage for coaches was once a small cheese factory which would have made an interesting comparison with the larger modern factory at Hartington.

This moorland road which runs across to Royal Cottage on the Leek road, crosses a watershed "par-excellence" for the hills are patterned with mountain streams running eastward to join the Manifold.

Turn right at the A53 and at the Travellers' Rest you will have completed a circuit of Staffordshire Moorland. The two rivers which form the basis of the two final sections of this book – the Dove and the Manifold – the rise in these parts. Just south of the Travellers' Rest is the source of the Manifold and to the north of it rises the Dove at appropriately Dove Head.

Returning to Buxton, Axe Edge now lies on your left and at 1,800 feet provides extensive views in most directions. If you like a quiz and play it the hard way by not looking at the answer try this:

Five well-known rivers rise around here; three already mentioned which flow to the North Sea eventually and two equally famous which flow to the Irish Sea though not necessarily under their original names.

They are listed in the Appendix

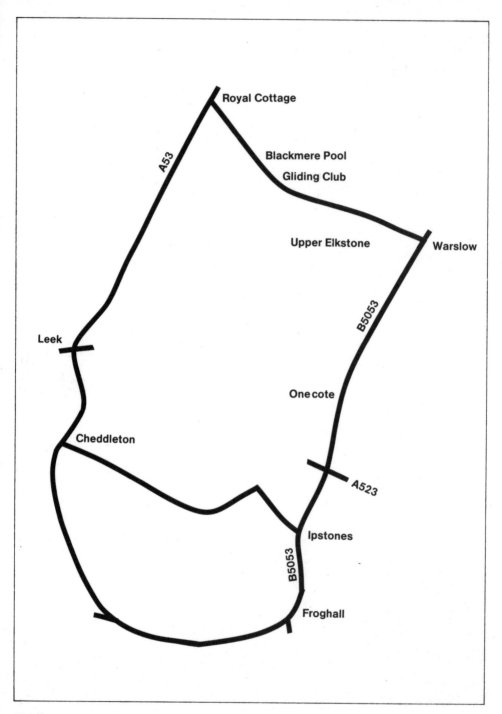

Royal Cottage

A53

Blackmere Pool

Gliding Club

Upper Elkstone

Warslow

B5053

Leek

Onecote

Cheddleton

A523

Ipstones

B5053

Froghall

28

7
Upper Elkstone, Warslow, Froghall, Cheddleton.

If you bisect the A53 at Royal Cottage and cross the edge of the DANGER AREA to Hulme End you plot the northern boundary of this section. There are aeronautical, sociological and even mythological aspects of this quite wild territory and the sad tale of a village that went 'dry'.

At Royal Cottage strike out across country on the road signed Warslow; that's the second left coming from Buxton, or the first right after the old school coming from Leek. Any likely danger lies in leaving the main road when the red flags are flying, but to date no traveller in these parts has yet been wounded – mortally or otherwise.

By remembering to keep right at each fork or crossroads you will eventually arrive at The Mermaid Inn and the legend of the lady who inhabited nearby Blackmere Pool. Opposite the Inn and on your forward route is a gliding club which operates most weekends.

Gliding can be a traffic hazard if you insist on looking and driving at the same time and so it is far better to park and observe one or two launchings and landings before proceeding along the narrower, minor roads to Elkstone. Upper is the first hamlet where the former Cock Inn is now a private residence – can you identify it? The church is still very much alive and it has one of those ancient two-decker pulpits with box pews to match. If it is open do take a look inside. Lower Elkstone is the scattered half lying nearer the B5053, where you turn left to visit Warslow if you have not previously done so. This is really an estate village, the Hall lying some distance up the road in the direction of Longnor. Again, the church is attractive with neat pine pews and some beautiful mosaic

Blackmere Pool

Staffordshire Gliding Club

Elkstone Church

work surrounding the stained glass windows by the altar. The large pew was originally built for the Squire and his family who are no longer in permanent residence at the Hall. A 'factory looking sort of building' (a local resident's description) on the edge of the village is the area school about which some controversy rages. In their infinite wisdom the Education Authority is closing some village primary schools and also operating a Middle School system to add to the confusion. Naturally the villagers concerned are resisting these attempts to 'weaken village life', as they vigorously contend it will.

From Warslow return on the B5053 in the same south-westerly direction, crossing first Warslow Brook, a tributary of the Manifold, then climbing towards Butterton whose church spire is a landmark in these parts. (The village is visited in Section 9.)

Onecote (locally Oncot) is the next village and the climb from here brings you to the boundary of the National Park with its familiar grit-stone wheel reminding you of that fact. At Bottom House you cross the A523, the Ashbourne road, and then a single track line which runs from the quarry at Cauldon Low to the main line. On the sky-line ahead of you is Ipstones Edge and beyond this you begin the descent to the village. In Ipstones, turn right by the shops and the Marquis of Granby and follow this winding road, past the church and out into the country.

This is a circular detour from Ipstones to Cheddleton which has been described as the most scenic run in Staffordshire. Keep left on this minor road to the left turn which will eventually bring you back to Ipstones, but for the moment keep ahead with the Basford and Cheddleton sign. Run on to the old station on the former North Staffordshire railway line which is being restored, hopefully, to enable steam trains to run again, and visit the railway museum. In Cheddleton village is the flint mill by the canal which currently is only open on Saturday and Sunday afternoons. Now return past the station and Basford crossroads to the right turn for Ipstones.

Moslee Hall, now a farm, was a former Jacobean house of the mid-seventeenth century and nearer Ipstones, by the two fishing ponds, is Belmont Hall lying off the road. The chapel-styled building was the outcome of an argument between Sneyd, who restored Ipstones church, and the clergy. When it was resolved the 'chapel' became a residence.

Back in the village you will again meet the B5053 where you turn right for Froghall. As you descend to this 'village' you will observe that it really only consists of Boltons Copper Wire Works. It was here that the cable for the first Atlantic telegraph service was manufactured. By turning left at the A52 and immediately left again, the two other attractions of Froghall are in view. The first being the Caldon Canal with its former wharf and now its horse-drawn narrow boat for trippers. The second is the picnic site and base for nature trails and country walks – an Information Board shows the lie of the land.

Churnet Valley Steam Railway Museum

Cheddleton Flint Mill

You could well take stock here for though this is the end of the line so to speak, there is so much more to see in these parts. The alternatives are that you return by the most convenient route and explore this area at a later date, or you continue with this present tour. Either way you should explore the Churnet Valley, Oakamoor, Alton village and Towers, then return perhaps via Ashbourne. The OS sheet 119 and leaflets from the Information Centre will enable you to see the Valley to advantage.

Caldon Canal

8
Chelmorton, Flagg, Monyash, Lathkill Dale, Arbor Low, Hartington, Beresford Dale, Earl Sterndale.

We begin this section on one of the most exhilarating roads in the whole of the north-west, the Roman Buxton/Ashbourne road, the A515. There is hardly space to do justice to a description of this run except to recommend it as a welcome alternative to the tedious A6 between Buxton and Derby.

Brierlow Bar is once again the springboard, but the quarries can be avoided by turning left on to the A5270 and then right with the Chelmorton sign along 'The Ditch'. This village, though outdone by Flash as the highest in The Peak, has a unique stone and slated telephone kiosk reputed to be the only one of its kind. It has pre-historic barrows on the summit of the flat topped Low, in fact, at 1400 feet the highest chambered tomb. Nearby Calton Hill is quarried for dolerite, a rock used in road building.

Flagg, the next village is the venue of the High Peak Hunt point to point races on Easter Tuesday, and from here Monyash is but a short drive away and both it and Flagg are surrounded by disused lead mines for which the area was once noted. The village of Monyash appears to have been scattered around the Bulls Head and the green and its history includes a market and fair charter, and a disputes court held, naturally in the Bulls Head.

Monyash

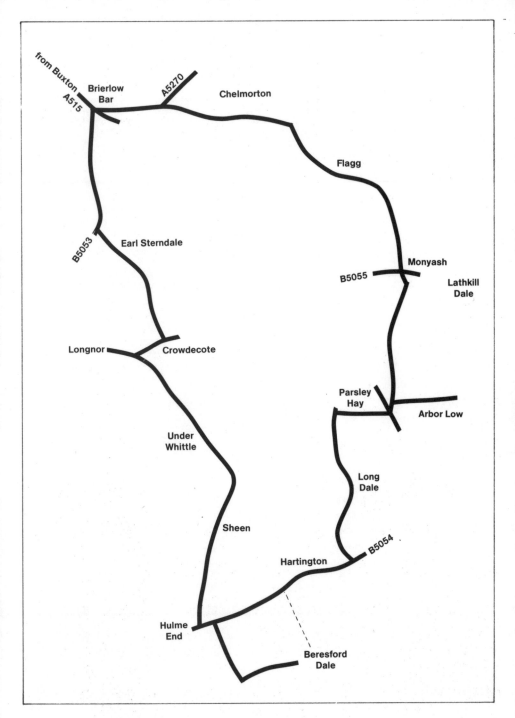

from Buxton

A515

Brierlow
Bar

A5270

Chelmorton

Flagg

B5053

Earl Sterndale

Monyash

B5055

Lathkill
Dale

Longnor

Crowdecote

Under
Whittle

Parsley
Hay

Arbor Low

Long
Dale

Sheen

B5054

Hartington

Hulme
End

Beresford
Dale

33

Arbor Low

The lovely Lathkill Dale lies to the east with One Ash Grange Farm at its head. This was for long the home of a Quaker family having associations with John Bright himself who took the name One Ash for his residence in Rochdale.

Travelling south from Monyash towards Parsley Hay and along the White Peak scenic route, the signs are for Arbor Low, described perhaps optimistically as 'The Stonehenge of Derbyshire'. This is a Bronze Age Stone Circle with the stones now lying prone which distinguishes it somewhat from Stonehenge. In fact, it has a closer affinity with the famous Avebury Ring, also in Wiltshire. The significance of this ring is religious rather than military though what cult practised its religion here it is not easy to speculate.

Parsley Hay

At the main Ashbourne road, take a sharp left and right with the Pilsbury sign for Parsley Hay, a one-time halt on the former railway line and now a picnic site and cycle hire centre. Briefly, the line from Buxton to Ashbourne ran through these parts and in fact the link with Hartington to Parsley Hay and the old High Peak Railway was the last section to be closed. In 1967 the death knoll sounded and in subsequent years the Peak Park Planning Board took over the track for one of their very popular Trails. Peak Pathfinder buses, hire cycles, trails for walkers, picnic sites for motorists, in fact almost everything to woo the city dweller into the countryside has been provided.

The road from Parsley Hay continues through the aptly named Long Dale to Hartington, one of those villages suffering under the strain of having 'picture postcard popularity'. It is a must for anyone touring the Peak District, not only for its own sake, but as a centre for touring lovely dales and precipitous gated roads. Its popularity with country lovers is such that the old hall east of the village is now a youth hostel. It stands today as a reminder of early seventeenth century house building. This is farming country and it comes as no surprise to learn that cheese is manufactured here – in fact the famous Stilton.

Hartington

Ecclesiastically, Hartington was once the centre of an important Parish and the church which dates from the thirteenth century is worth a little of your time. Like most popular places Hartington has two faces: the one reserved for weekends when tourists invade the tea rooms and the village shops and the workaday face of any weekday morning when it is just another village getting on with its normal routine.

It will be more convenient to explore Beresford Dale in this section and there are two approaches. On foot the route lies by path which strategically commences by the public conveniences and runs from the village to the east bank of the Dove. By car you enter Staffordshire over the river bridge, then follow the lanes left to the approach which passes the caravan site. Cotton and Walton are the names synonymous with the Dove and Beresford Dale is not only a delightful place in its own right, but holds a number of mementoes of these famous fishermen. Cotton's Cave and Prospect Tower are on private land on the Staffordshire side of the river and also hidden among the trees is the fishing house built by Cotton in 1674, and again on private land.

The Fishing Temple

Two minor roads run northwards off the B5054 as you leave Hartington and the Dove and both take you to Sheen, one of those long straggling villages with no apparent centre. On the stretch between here and Longnor is a parking spot with views across to Pilsbury with ruins of a Norman 'motte and Bailey' castle. Before Longnor is an awkward right turn which doubles back to Crowdecote, a village which hangs on a hill. The Packhorse Inn is so named because of its associations with that mode of transport. In contrast the inn sign at Earl Sterndale has a more macabre connotation. The Quiet Woman is depicted by a headless female! Curiously, or perhaps sadly, the village church was actually bombed during the last War. The view from the road leading out of the village takes in those twin peaks of Parkhouse and Chrome and on the horizon, Axe Edge Moor.

From here to Brierlow Bar and the return to Buxton, the road once more passes those gaping quarries. The passengers (but please not the driver) can always close their eyes!

By following the circuit in a clockwise direction described above, all the attractions of this section are visited. There is yet more of the Dove and the Manifold to come in the two final sections.

9
Manifold Valley

Knowing that these final sections of the book take you into
the Manifold Valley and Dovedale you might be forgiven for
thinking that we have indeed suggested that 'the best is
yet to come'. The Manifold Valley and Dovedale vie with
each other in friendly rivalry, but fortunately their
characteristics are not absolutely identical and they each
in turn offer the tourist a delightful experience. This
particular section concerns itself with the Manifold running
down from Hulme End to its junction with the Dove at Ilam.
The route for both walkers and motorists follows the track
of the former light railway, though walkers are favoured
with sections which are closed to traffic.

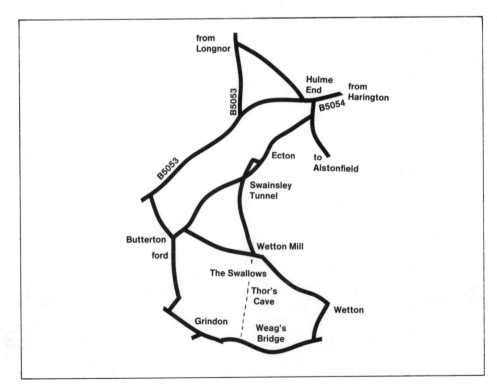

From Hulme End take the first right off the Alstonfield road for Ecton with its history of mining for copper, as the spire on the peculiar folly will confirm. The old mine workings are dangerous and should not be explored, even supposing you actually locate them. The social, economic and industrial histories of the place are worth examining more closely with two pence per hour for men and two pence per day for twelve year old sorters being the 'going rate'.

The whole drive is nostalgic and one wonders whether the valley would have suffered the fate of more popular places had the light railway still been running. To locate Swainsley Tunnel and the valley proper, turn right towards the picnic spot and left to enter the tunnel, (ignore the Butterton sign and follow Wetton Mill). For children and adults still young in heart this is an exciting introduction to the charm of the Manifold Valley and at Wetton Mill a halt should be made to plot further progress. It is at Wetton Mill during the busy season that a comparison with Dovedale can be made. There may be problems with parking and long queues for ice-cream so the strategy is to visit popular beauty spots on quieter weekdays or out of season when they can be appreciated in comparative calm. The walk, or rather climb, up to Thor's Cave can be made from here. Continue along the old railway track where vehicles

Wetton Mill

are now prohibited and soon across left you will see the path which leads up to the Cave. The ascent is not too difficult but a gentler approach is available from the road leading out of the valley, though you have a parking problem on this stretch. The view from the Cave is ample reward for the exertions of the climb and the experience should not be missed if at all possible.

By continuing along the track on foot, you can rendezvous with a car at the next public road, Weags Bridge, and this is why the onward route should be considered whilst picnicking at Wetton Mill.

Also on the stretch from the car park to Thor's Cave is an interesting geological phenomenon 'The Swallows'. Here in dry weather the river disappears for about four miles to reappear in the grounds of Ilam Hall (see Section 10). This of course, is due to the porous nature of the limestone and the River Lathkill is another such example. The accompanying sketch map depicts the two routes which are now available to you depending perhaps on what remains of the time or your ultimate onward route. By climbing out of the valley on the Wetton road, you pass the second approach to Thor's Cave and arrive in Wetton village. Now, keeping right all the way you again descend to the valley at Weags Bridge, where the walkway meets the roadway and another parking and picnic spot is provided. By climbing rather trickily out you arrive at Grindon, with its prominent church spire. The severe winter of 1947 is recalled inside the church by a memorial to an air crew who lost their lives when bringing relief supplies.

Grindon is one of the more isolated hamlets of these parts and like neighbouring Butterton is above the 1000 feet contour. After Grindon, turn right by the 'phone box to drop down to Butterton by the next turn left. In the bottom you cross a ford which is normally negotiable and which has a high pavement for pedestrians if anyone wishes to take photographs as the car splashes through. When climbing up the village take the narrower right fork to the church and the pub, then re-join the road out by bearing left. Note that the road right by the school is the approach to Wetton Mill, thus completing the circuit. The more direct route is to the B5053, the Warslow/Longnor/Hartington road which lies just to the west of Butterton village, but if the children want another trip through the tunnel then you will have to descend to the valley again, and return via Ecton.

A word about the Peak Pathfinders Bus Service would not be inappropriate here. The service is sponsored by the National Park people in an endeavour to reduce traffic congestion in the Park and adjacent areas. For a quite nominal charge whole families can be transported to the majority of the well-known beauty spots without the tedium of having to drive yourself. A fairly generous frequency of service enables the walker, picnicker, or whoever to enjoy a full day in one or more of these delightful places. In spite of the 'pull' of the family car, this is an alternative which should not be overlooked for there is no driver to miss the scenery — everyone gets a look in!

Thor's Cave

Well Dressings

The origin of well dressings is not absolutely clear, being either pagan or a token of gratitude for pure water in times of plague. The art is a specialised one and occupies the villagers for many weeks before the actual ceremony. A Biblical scene or church are the more usual subjects and the occasion is often supported by other events in the village — a fair or carnival.

Dates are usually quoted for the Blessing ceremony and it is advisable to see them as soon as they are on view when they are at their best.

10
Tissington, Ashbourne, Dovedale, Ilam, Alstonfield.

Section 10 is 'Dale country' with the choice between Wolfscote, Biggin, Mill, Hall, Lin and Dove. They range from the small and sometimes missed to the larger and more popular, and they offer the energetic plenty of scope for walking. Well dressing, a Derbyshire custom of considerable charm is very much a feature of these parts. (See the notes opposite)

Tissington is as pretty a village as its name suggests and for many is 'the' well dressing village. It has a distinct advantage in that its wells are the first to be decorated each year (around Ascension time). There are numerous publications on well dressing, usually available in villages where the ceremony is taking place. Again, the Peak Calendar for the year quotes all the dates and locations. Tissington's other association is with the newly developed Trail along the track of the old railway — a former milk run. Walk if you care to as far as Ashbourne, and rendezvous there.

Tissington Hall

40

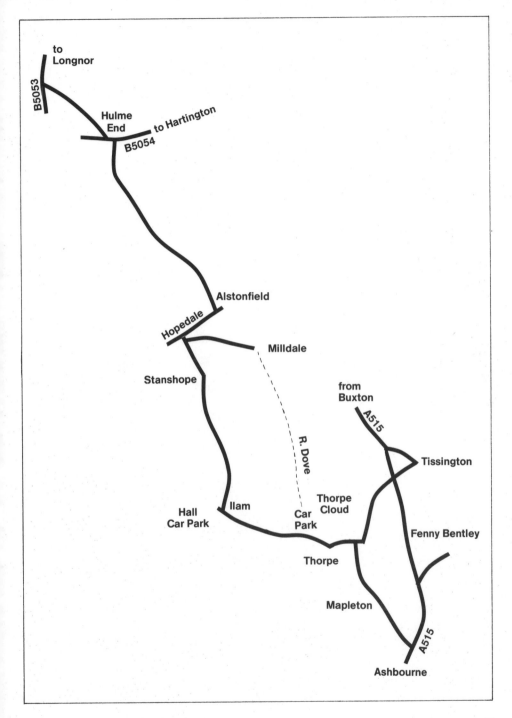

Since the village lies east of the Ashbourne road it should be visited first before embarking on the circuit of the Dales. Two possibilities are now open to you: a run down to Ashbourne, particularly if someone has taken the Trail, or the direct route from Tissington village to Thorpe and Ilam. Ashbourne will demand quite a fair portion of your time, it is a town for parking in and browsing through and has a very useful Information Centre. The new one-way system might fox you but whichever route you use you should exit up the Buxton road to the top of the market square, and turn left into Union Street. Your onward route is now signed Mapleton and Okeover, and you first pass the car park for the Tissington Trail before continuing to Mapleton and then Thorpe. From this village one can walk to the famous stepping stones by following a path behind the Peveril of the Peak Hotel, the northern side of Thorpe Cloud and finally Lin Dale to the Dove and the stones. By road you must cross the river and the boundary and follow the Staffordshire bank of the Dove to the car park. Should you drive right up to the stones, parking is prohibited so that walking is in this instance Hobson's choice.

Ashbourne Market

Opposite: Dovedale

Ilam Rock, Dovedale

Castle Rocks, Dovedale

Cloud, old English 'clud' means rock or hill and Thorpe Cloud is technically misnamed for it is more of a ridge than a cone as a view from the riverside will reveal. Almost a thousand acres of Dovedale are in the safe keeping of the National Trust, though this in itself will not guarantee its survival as 'a place as noble as anywhere in Greece or Switzerland', Lord Byron's description. It suffers the handicap of being popular with tourists and for this reason and others, no longer offers the peace and tranquillity of former years. Nevertheless, the Dale should be visited, at weekends if you like crowds or on a quieter weekday if not. Its beauty is particularly accentuated in spring, autumn and after a winter's snow. Whilst scenically the 1979 winter was magnificent, sadly it will be remembered for the hardships it caused. The river is to fishing what Lords is to cricket or Wembley to soccer, and both Cotton and Walton are revered and remembered in a variety of ways. Walking northwards on the Derbyshire bank of the river, a path takes you to Mill Dale, almost three miles upstream, and here is another convenient spot for a rendezvous where the road from Alsop-en-le-Dale to Alstonfield passes close by.

The duplicating of so many well-known Derbyshire landmarks could be confusing for the map of Dovedale reveals such familiar names as: Jacob's Ladder, Tissington Spires, Dove Holes, Lover's Leap and the Twelve Apostles. These names have been given to the curiously shaped limestone tors and spires and you could walk part way up the Dale to view just a few of them, and then return to the car park.

At this stage in the book it seems hardly necessary to point out that the Dove from Axe Edge to its approach to the Trent is the county boundary. Its tributary, the Manifold, forms a junction between Thorpe and Ilam, two villages of contrasting styles. Ilam is a model estate village built in the mid-nineteenth century for one Jesse Watts-Russell. A Gothic styled Hall and the lovely grounds have belonged to the National Trust since the 1930's, and there is parking, a caravan site and a country park, all catering again for the tourist. It is in the grounds of Ilam Hall that the Manifold reappears after its subterranean journey through 'The Swallows'. The National Trust now has one of its attractive shops in the Hall and the whole scene is remarkably peaceful after the bustle of neighbouring Dovedale. From Ilam travel north through Stanshope to the T junction and the right turn for Alstonfield, but at the next right by the Watts-Russell Arms, turn right and run down to Mill Dale, which is the northern end of the walk through Dovedale. This is a tiny hamlet which fortunately does not lend itself to any twentieth century development and is a popular reference point, particularly for walkers.

Return to the pub and up to Alstonfield, where the church, in common with many that are visited by tourists, has prepared an interesting leaflet, 'a simple guide to St Peter's Church, Alstonfield'. The Cotton pew and the pulpit are the main attractions. The village also boasts a curiously shaped gnarled tree opposite the George Hotel and an art and craft shop.

To complete this section, leave Alstonfield in the direction of Hulme End where you meet the B5054 and again, turn right for Hartington and then Buxton.

Ilam Village

Appendix

Adlington Hall
Open Good Friday to early October on Sundays and Bank Holidays (also Wednesdays and Saturdays during July and August) from 2.30pm to 6pm.
Telephone Prestbury (3) 829206

Gawsworth
Open late March to late October 2 to 6pm daily.
Telephone North Rode (026 03) 456

Lyme Hall
March and October, Sundays 1 to 4pm
    Tuesday to Saturday conducted
    tours only at 2, 3 and 4pm.
April to September, Sundays and Bank
    Holidays 1 to 5.30pm. Tuesday to
    Saturday 2 to 5pm.
Closed Mondays (except Bank
    Holidays) and November to
    February.
Telephone Disley (066 32) 2023

Brindley Mill
Mill Street, Leek.
Open weekends and Bank Holiday Mondays from Easter to the end of October 2 to 5pm.

Churnet Valley Steam Railway Museum
May to September, Monday to Saturday
    12 to 5.30pm. Sundays and Bank
    Holidays 11am to 6.30pm.
October to April, Sundays only 12 to
    5.30pm.
Telephone Churnet Side (0538) 360522

Coombs Valley Nature Reserve
Near Leek
Open Tuesday, Thursday and weekends.

Froghall Wharf Passenger Service
Foxt Road, Froghall, Nr. Cheadle
2½ hour trips every Thursday and
    Sunday at 2pm.
3½ hour evening meal trips on the
    first and third Saturday of the
    Summer months.
For further information and details of private charters telephone Ipstones (053 871) 486

Five Rivers Question page 27.
Answer: The Dove, Manifold, Goyt, Wye and Dane.

Poole's Cavern
Green Lane, Buxton
Open daily (except Wednesdays) from Easter to October.
Telephone Buxton (0298) 6978

Rudyard Lake Sailing Club
Telephone Newcastle (0782) 616655

Staffordshire Gliding Club
Telephone Blackshaw (053 834) 369 or Poynton (709) 3747

Ashbourne Tourist Information Centre
13 The Market Place
Telephone 03355 3666

Buxton Tourist Information Centre
St. Ann's Well, The Crescent
Telephone 0298 5106

Leek Tourist Information Centre
St. Edward St.
Telephone 0538 385509

Macclesfield Tourist Information Centre
Town Hall, Market St.
Telephone 0625 21955

Buxton Youth Hostel
Sherbrook Lodge, Harpur Hill Rd.
Telephone 0298 2287

Hartington Youth Hostel
Telephone 029884 463

Ilam Youth Hostel
Telephone 033529 212

Meerbrook Youth Hostel
Telephone 053834 244

Windgather Youth Hostel
Telephone 06633 2153

Youlgrave Youth Hostel
Telephone 062986 518

Maps
White Peak 1:25000 Outdoor Leisure
    Map.
Peak District "One Inch" Tourist Map.
Buxton, Matlock and Dove Dale
    1:50000, sheet 119.

Opposite: Conksbury Bridge